CENTRAL MARKET:
Cornerstone of the Lancaster Community

CENTRAL MARKET:
Cornerstone of the Lancaster Community

Linda S. Aleci
With photographs by Richard K. Kent

The Friends of Central Market
Lancaster, Pennsylvania, 2009

Front Cover: A view of Central Market from Penn Square prior to 1924 courtesy of LancasterHistory.org.
Back Cover: Central Market, 1942. Photo by Marjory Collins.
Photos of Central Market wares courtesy of Melissa Carroll.

Printed by Cadmus Communications, Lancaster, Pennsylvania

ISBN 978-0-615-32113-4
Library of Congress Control Number: 2009936872

Published by The Friends of Central Market
P.O. Box 1623, Lancaster, PA 17608-1623
www.friendsofcentralmarket.org

❧ Contents

❧ *Foreword*

The story of this book:
The Library of Congress Local Legacies Project

In 1999, the Library of Congress launched The Local Legacies Project 2000, an unprecedented initiative in which citizens across the nation documented a traditional activity or aspect of their community that has been important to America's grassroots heritage. As part of this effort, The Friends of Central Market was asked to document the significance of Central Market, on behalf of Lancaster and the nation. Joined by photographers, historians, market standholders, and many community members, The Friends of Central Market worked for a year, recovering and documenting the tradition of "market"—the coming together of Lancaster's residents, farmers, and food producers to buy and sell in Central Market for nearly 300 years. The Local Legacies submission also provided the catalyst in October 2000 for the exhibition "Central Market and the Tradition of Market in Lancaster, Pennsylvania," curated by Linda Aleci, Richard K. Kent, and Robert Lowing, in The Chestnut House Gallery directly across from the market building.

The Local Legacies Project marked the beginning of a continuing effort by The Friends of Central Market to understand and protect this extraordinary monument to community and place by bringing its history to light. With the Lancaster County Historical Society, the organization was instrumental in developing the exhibition "Market*Place*: Lancaster

Opposite page: Saife's Middle Eastern Foods and owner Omar Hussein represent one of many cultural traditions that make Central Market a true reflection of Lancaster County's diversity. 1999.

PHOTO: RICHARD K. KENT

Market basket on her arm, an Amish woman walks through Penn Square, circa 1920.

Central Market and the Making of Community," the first scholarly exhibition on Central Market, created in 2005 to commemorate the 275th anniversary of the market's founding. *Central Market: Cornerstone of the Lancaster Community* continues this tradition. Produced by The Friends of Central Market with financial support from the Central Market Trust, it honors the first major campaign to restore the Central Market house and the effort to bring back its original character as a farmers' market. Much of the text for *Central Market: Cornerstone of the Lancaster Community* is drawn from the materials submitted to the Library of Congress and edited to fit the format of this book. In addition, some new content has been written in collaboration with The Friends of Central Market to bring the narrative up to the present. The book design is the creation of Mike Abel of Abel/Savage Marketing & Communications, whose experience and expertise was invaluable to the project.

The original submission to the Library of Congress included a selection of historic photographs kindly provided by the Lancaster County Historical Society, and a set of 24 black-and-white portraits of standholders and interior views of the market made by Richard K. Kent in 1999. Many of these appear in the present volume, with some additional photographs obtained from the past decade. The beauty of these images can be found in the wealth of information they contain. Past and present, old and new, what is remembered and cherished as well as what is forgotten: they are an invitation to look closely and see the market with new eyes.

Spoken in dialogue with the images are the words of the people on market. One priority of the original Local Legacies project was to document the individuals who had been on market the longest; they are the human repository of the market's history. Some of that material came from older interviews found in published sources; some was collected as part of the Central Market Oral History Project, which records the memories and stories of Central Market standholders past and present, and of the people who have been part of their lives as market-goers. Many of these individuals have since retired or, in some cases, have passed on, but they will always be a part of the market's story. Given that Central Market is now concluding its first decade of the twenty-first century, the voices of children at market and a younger generation of market-goers and standholders have been introduced to give us a glimpse of the market's future.

In this new form, *Central Market: Cornerstone of the Lancaster Community* intends to convey a sense of market that is at once historical, modern, commemorative and intimate. The book does not pretend that market is a universal experience or a timeless moment: the sum of images and voices creates the picture of a particular market that was born with Lancaster itself. Its lifetime is Lancaster's: generations of people, objects, sights and habits make up its character. Past and present, living and dead, urban and rural, the continuity of these elements is what holds together the enduring fabric of this community.

The Library of Congress officially declared Lancaster Central Market "a National Local Legacy" in May 2000. It was so honored for preserving and sustaining the most traditional and historically significant feature of community life in Lancaster—the activity of market-going—and for preserving Lancaster as one of America's original market towns.

—Linda S. Aleci

Welcome to Central Market

❧ Welcome to Central Market

Jacob H. Thomas hands over a ham
to 3-year-old Billy Hess. 1946.
PHOTO: LANCASTERHISTORY.ORG

Going to market is a cherished tradition that connects Lancaster County's two defining characteristics: the working farms that form the bedrock of the county's economy, and the vibrant urban center that is the focal point of its commerce and culture. Neither could exist without the other, and every Central Market shopper and standholder is an essential part of this story.

Lancaster's Central Market is one of America's most beloved and beautiful markets precisely because it has always been exactly that—a vibrant, working marketplace. Lancastrians have been coming to the market square in the heart of Lancaster to buy local farm products since the early 1700s, making Central Market the oldest continuously operating municipal market in the United States. Because of this rich heritage and the distinctively handsome market house built by the people of Lancaster in 1889, Central Market is also one of the city's most-visited tourist attractions—just as it was in the nineteenth century.

Most people think of Central Market only as a building. And a grand building it is, a magisterial presence that presides over the downtown, a landmark constructed on the site of Lancaster's original marketplace.

Opposite page: Ernie Thomas, of C. H. Thomas and Sons—no relation to Jacob Thomas, above—was the fourth generation of his family to sell fresh meats on market. 1999.
PHOTO: RICHARD K. KENT

1

"Market" is also an activity, one that has both sustained and defined a community. This book explores all of these elements. *An Enduring Public Place* looks at aspects of the Market in the context of Lancaster, its agricultural lands, and the architecture of the market house. *A Vital Activity* explores the power of the living marketplace as a social and economic environment. *The Community of Market* is about the people who have created it, and are even now creating it anew.

As a place, as an activity and as a community, Central Market defines downtown Lancaster and, in many ways, the whole of Lancaster County. It serves as an enduring testament to the region's agricultural past and present; and as a dynamic, living expression of Lancaster County's uniqueness. It is a hopeful beacon for the future.

While Central Market's impact is primarily local, its importance extends much farther. It represents an American tradition of market-going that has been largely lost as local markets have given way to supermarkets and warehouse stores that break the link between producer and consumer. Yet Central Market is much more than a quaint reminder of fading traditions. As we look for better ways to bring food to our tables—ways that have less adverse environmental impact, that support a struggling farm population, that better nourish communities as well as bodies—Central Market and the county that has supported it for nearly 300 years represent a rare and valuable model for towns and cities everywhere.

Few Lancaster County residents may stop to think about the broader implications of their public market heritage, but it is demonstrated every time they shop in Central Market's aisles or sell products from its stalls. This is the common ground on which the community was born, and to which it returns every market day.

Central Market is much more than a quaint reminder of a traditional market. As we look for better ways to bring food to our tables— ways that have less adverse environmental impact, that support a struggling farm population, that better nourish our communities as well as our bodies—Central Market and the county that has supported it for nearly 300 years represent a valuable model for towns and cities everywhere.

ABOVE PHOTO: MARJORY COLLINS, NOVEMBER, 1942. LIBRARY OF CONGRESS, PRINTS & PHOTOGRAPHS DIVISION, FSA-OWI COLLECTION, LCUSW3-011041-E

An Enduring Public Place

Central Market: Cornerstone of the Lancaster Community

❦ An Enduring Public Place

Sometimes, at just the right moment of the day, sunlight streams through the market's high dormer windows and pierces the great interior space. At times like these, the beauty of Central Market's architecture comes alive. Its power as an enduring public place seems most tangible.

Central Market has evolved from a sprawling outdoor array of "shambles" to a stately market house. But the essential character of the place cannot be described simply in terms of its appearance. It is explained by its purpose. Both the original land grant and the royal charter clearly define Central Market's function, one it was intended to fulfill in perpetuity. Deeded to the citizens of Lancaster, to be maintained on their behalf by the municipality, Central Market was meant to ensure a continual supply of good food for the new settlement. In other words, the marketplace is a monument to a principle of justice—*salus populi*, existing for the good of the people. This principle comes to life in the everyday practice of going to market, the place where food, commerce, and civic life commingle.

As a public market, Central Market defines both a common ground and food as a common good, something that must be shared by all of us

The curb market along South Duke Street, circa 1925.
PHOTO: LANCASTERHISTORY.ORG

Opposite page: Two rays of sunshine illuminate the market house as farmer-standholder Earl Groff, right, discusses his homegrown produce offerings with a busy shopper. 1999.
PHOTO: RICHARD K. KENT

and so binds us together. The marketplace is a space held in common by all manner of people, for the purpose of gathering to engage in one of the most basic and essential of human activities—the buying and selling of provisions.

This may explain why Central Market has stood the test of time, and how its history has been translated into a viable modern institution.

❦ Beginnings

"As we leave Chester County, and pass through the range of hills called Mine Ridge, the great county of Lancaster, in all its glory, expands before the eye. An intelligent Englishman called this county the 'garden of America,' and a view of it from this position will fully justify the propriety of this compliment. It is, without a doubt, the garden of this glorious Union, and there are few spots in this wide world, which could present a nobler scene to the eye than is here afforded... The whole of the country is, therefore, in the highest state of cultivation; and in the economy which characterizes the general agricultural system, there is probably not a more prolific region in the United States."[1]

Lancaster's history is filled with many glowing observations, like this one written by Eli Bowen in 1852, describing its agricultural bounty and the thriving market activity it spawned. They make clear that the rise of Lancaster as a market town was made possible, first and foremost, by the fertile farmland that surrounded it. Distinct from other early settlements, Lancaster was the hub of "a large unbroken body of the richest land in Pennsylvania, or in any other of the Atlantic States," as Anne Royall wrote in 1828.[2]

Lancaster's location played an important role in the establishment of a thriving market. It was situated on the King's Highway (now King Street), the first westward route from Philadelphia to the continental interior and one of the major transportation routes of the region. The future of the not-yet-born settlement was forecast by this strategic placement when on May 16, 1730, Andrew Hamilton and his wife, Ann, conveyed from their private estate a 120-square-foot lot in the northwest corner of the

The rise of Lancaster as a market town was made possible, first and foremost, by the fertile farmland that surrounded the developing settlement.

"In every respect [the Lancaster market is] equal to that of Philadelphia. Every article for the table abounds in the Lancaster market, and brought in neat order."

— Anne Royall, visiting Lancaster in 1828

intersection of the King's Highway and Lancaster's main north-south road (today's Queen Street) for use as a public market. Taking its place with the courthouse as the actual and symbolic heart of the settlement, the market was both accessible for commerce and highly visible as a sign of a vibrant civic life.

Little is known about that first market. Before roughly the middle of the eighteenth century it was simply an open plot of land where farmers could sell from the backs of their wagons and carts. However modest it may have been initially, the early market paved the way for Lancaster's designation as a market town—a coveted status that had a lasting impact on the character and position of the city. When King George II of England formally chartered the borough in 1742, he decreed that it should hold "two markets in each week, that is to say one market on Wednesday, and one market on Saturday in every week of the year for ever in the lot of ground already agreed upon for that purpose and granted for that use."

Soon after, the first market regulations were issued, and in October 1742 market stalls were created—"six stalls, eight feet front each on King Street and five feet deep, and the rest as many as may be wanted to be laid back to the north part of the market place."

Lancaster curb market, circa 1909.

🌱 The market grows

From Lancaster's earliest days, the city's urban prosperity and the county's agricultural wealth were inseparably linked. This made it imperative that the city leaders ensured the market would continue to meet the needs of a growing population and economy. By 1757, Lancaster's burgesses had erected a market building, probably only a rudimentary structure consisting of rows of stalls covered with a roof. Later it was redone in oak shingles and had a brick floor. After many years of repairs and additions, the market "shed" was replaced by the new Town Hall (now the Heritage Center) in 1795, and a brick arcade fronting on King Street was built adjoining the west end of the Town Hall in 1798. These alterations had the effect of defining the marketplace and transforming it into a kind of square. In 1815, more market sheds were built just north of the open-sided structure. When Lancaster was chartered as a city three years later, an ordinance delineated the limits of an expanded market square to include the market house, the public space north of it, West King Street as far as Prince Street, "and the whole of Centre Square" (now Penn Square). Passing through Lancaster in 1828, Anne Royall visited and much admired this market, pronouncing it "in every respect equal to that of Philadelphia. Every article for the table abounds in the Lancaster market, and brought in neat order" (although she was put off by the appearance and smell of "Dutch" [*Deitsch* or Pennsylvania German] cheese—perhaps referring to cup cheese, which she described as "a great curiosity").

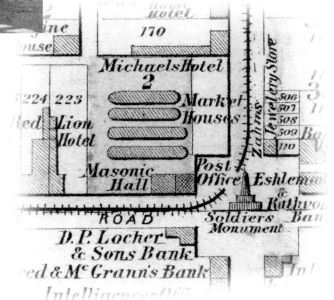

A fruit vendor on the curb market, circa 1909.
PHOTO: LANCASTERHISTORY.ORG

The 1875 Everts & Stewart atlas shows four open-air market sheds northwest of Centre (Penn) Square. These are probably the same structures shown in the photo on page 12. For shoppers' convenience, a trolley line runs through the square from King Street to Queen. The evolution of the market is shown in greater detail in Appendix II starting on page 78.

PHOTO: LANCASTERHISTORY.ORG

…four long, narrow market sheds occupied the site, as well as separate fish stands and "the Short Market," which included a coffee house.

Central Market: Cornerstone of the Lancaster Community

As the community's population continued to grow, the city in 1854 purchased additional land around the market square, cleared the existing buildings and erected several open-sided shed buildings. Between 1856 and 1875, four long, narrow market sheds occupied the site, as well as separate fish stands and "the Short Market," which included a coffee house. By 1876 a rag-tag assembly of 280 stalls, enclosed by two large wooden buildings, and 220 exterior market stands filled the market square.

Opposite page: A rare photographic view of the sheds of Central Market, circa 1856–1875.

PHOTO: LANCASTERHISTORY.ORG

❦ *Lancaster responds to a growing threat*

The present Central Market house was built in response to a growing threat to the municipality. By the middle of the nineteenth century, financial speculators began to form private market companies to compete with city-owned public markets, a practice that was especially rampant in Pennsylvania and regarded with some horror. By 1888, Lancaster had four privately held markets—the Northern, Western, Eastern, and Southern markets—impressive buildings compared to the municipal Central Market. Private investors had tried to lease the public market square in 1873, but Lancaster's

Central Market's competition, top: Northern Market, 1872, North Queen and Walnut Streets. Plans drawn by J. H. Baumgardner. Rebuilt 1884. John Evans, architect. Demolished 1958.
Above left: Western Market, 1883, 528 West Orange Street. Jacob Nordorf, designer. J. Adam Burger, contractor.
Above right: Eastern Market, 1883, East King and South Shippen Streets. John Evans, architect. J. Adam Burger, contractor.
Right: Southern Market, 1888, South Queen and Vine Streets. C. Emlen Urban, architect. J. Adam Burger, contractor.

ALL PHOTOS: LANCASTERHISTORY.ORG

mayor was outraged, and the city set in motion a public works project that would yield the defining fixture in downtown Lancaster for more than a century—and it remains so today.

Not to be outdone by entrepreneurs and their well-appointed market houses, the city contracted with James Warner, an English architect well-known for his church buildings and engineering of large roof spans, to design the new municipal market house. In March of 1889, his plans were approved, and ground was broken in late June. The building, much-anticipated as the most modern, sanitary, and well-constructed of Lancaster's market houses, with exceptionally attractive and functional stalls, was finished in an astonishing five months and dedicated in late autumn as a civic symbol of the public trust. When it was open for public inspection on the evening of Tuesday, November 5, the city newspapers reported that "hundreds of people visited the beautiful building."

By the end of World War I, when most of America's public markets were closing (only 237 municipal markets in 128 cities survived in 1918), Lancaster was one of the few places bucking the trend. In fact, by 1950, Lancaster had not one but two public markets. After leasing the Southern Market for 23 years to accommodate the farmers displaced when the curb markets closed, the city purchased it. Southern Market operated as a second municipal market until 1985, when it closed its doors, leaving Central Market to carry on the city's market tradition.

Opposite page: Marjory Collins, a photographer for the Office of War Information, visited Central Market on a rainy day in November, 1942. At this time Eberly's Restaurant occupied the ground floor of the southeast tower.

Central Market: Cornerstone of the Lancaster Community

✣ A living legacy

Like most historic buildings, the Central Market house has not remained unscathed over its long life. Particularly in the 1960s and 1970s there was great pressure to modernize the building so it could compete with supermarkets springing up around the edge of the city. Renovation proposals invariably produced a healthy debate over their appropriateness and fidelity to the original structure.

Today the market house stands intact, although alterations have been made to the interior and exterior. The most significant of these occurred in the 1970s, with the addition of a mezzanine level with toilets and an office that was built into the interior of the southeast corner along with a brick trash shed erected on the north side. Also in the seventies, the five arched windows on the south gable were covered, and recessed doorways and alcoves created around the periphery. A network of incandescent "can" fixtures was hung in large rectangular frames from the building's posts and trusses. On the outside, the cartways and curbs were eliminated, the fish stands removed from the north side, and bollards placed around the perimeter of the building to make a combined vehicular and pedestrian area. The original slate roof had already been replaced in 1960 with asphalt shingles.

In 2005, in conjunction with the county and the Lancaster Chamber

Vendors in the new market house placed great value on being a "good neighbor," with four farmers sharing a 12-foot stand.

PHOTOS: MARJORY COLLINS, NOVEMBER, 1942. LIBRARY OF CONGRESS, PRINTS & PHOTOGRAPHS DIVISION, FSA-OWI COLLECTION, LCUSW3-011005-E, LCUSW3-011010-E, LCUSW3-011033-E, LCUSW3-011008-E

Opposite page: Central Market shoppers who raise their eyes toward the roof are rewarded with a different perspective of the market house's architectural splendor. 1999.
PHOTO: RICHARD K. KENT

of Commerce and Industry, the city developed a Central Market Master Plan that called for the creation of the Central Market Trust, a non-profit entity charged with the operation of the market, which would continue to be owned by the city. The plan recognized that significant capital improvements had not been made since the work in the early 1970s, and a program of ongoing maintenance and repair was greatly needed. The Central Market Trust was formed in 2006 with a board of community leaders who oversee the management of the market as well as its upkeep and improvement.

The Trust launched a $7 million capital campaign in 2007 to perform basic mechanical system upgrades and maintenance work. The plan called for improved lighting and security; better restrooms; and upgrades to the roof, windows, doors, and the mezzanine. Electrical and plumbing systems were to be replaced and modernized, and the gateways and streets leading to and around the market were to be improved.

That same year, The Friends of Central Market collaborated with the Historic Preservation Trust of Lancaster County and commissioned a preservation development and planning document for Central Market. Funded in part by the Lancaster County Community Foundation, the planning document comprises the work of a professional team of architects, a market scholar, and consultants in the fields of public market planning, historic preservation, urban planning, and public policy. It establishes, for the first time, a framework for the care of the building and site based on historical research and architectural fieldwork, and lays out the core principles for fostering design compatibility in instances of rehabilitation to Central Market and the market square.

Opposite page: A Central Market patron since he was a child, Denny Kerek, right, passes on the tradition to his son, Chip, and grandson, Owen, at The Herb Shop. 1999.

PHOTO: RICHARD K. KENT

An Enduring Public Place

Lancaster Central Market House, James Warner, architect, 1889.
East-West Cross Section (looking South).

DRAWING: GEMMA DE LA FUENTE, PADEN DE LA FUENTE, ARCHITECTS

CENTRAL MARKET DETAIL PHOTOS: GEMMA DE LA FUENTE, PADEN DE LA FUENTE, ARCHITECTS

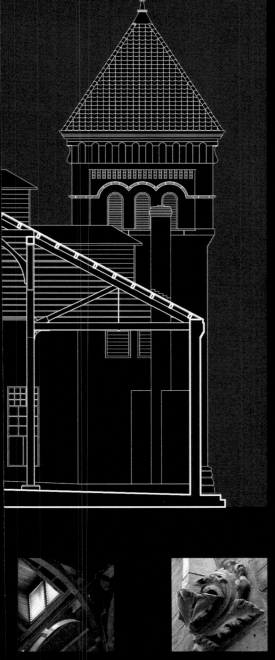

The Market House: A Rare Architectural Jewel

Built in 1889 and placed on the National Register of Historic Places in 1972, the Central Market building today is a rare surviving example of a nineteenth-century market house, a building type that once was common in southeastern Pennsylvania.

Because the Central Market had the highest civic significance, James Warner used a simple design that contrasts with the architecturally elaborate private market houses, multifunctional buildings that incorporated storefronts, meeting rooms, sometimes apartments and restaurants. Central Market is a single-use building, its unusual L-shaped footprint directly reflecting the combined area of the 1876 market structures. It fills the market square, resting on an imposing base of rusticated red sandstone and framed by robust twin towers at its front corners, each measuring 72 feet high.

Thirteen sets of double doors open into a space as dramatic as that of any cathedral. A vast roof carried by a network of timber and iron trusses on just 20 columns covers a 20,000

square foot floor. Twenty-two dormer windows pierce the roof, part of a natural ventilation system designed to draw the stale air and odors up from the floor.

The building originally held 160 stalls for farmers, and 72 for the butchers, whose stands were relegated to the periphery of the interior walls. The fishmongers—20 in all—were assigned to sell outdoors on the cooler north side of the market, where the great roof overhang was designed to shelter them and shade their products. The number of tenants that could be accommodated inside was actually much greater than the number of stalls. Before the alterations were made in the 1970s, the aisles were narrower and vendors stood four to a 12-foot-long stand, each allocated a 3-foot selling surface, ensuring the need for being a "good neighbor," as one standholder recalled.

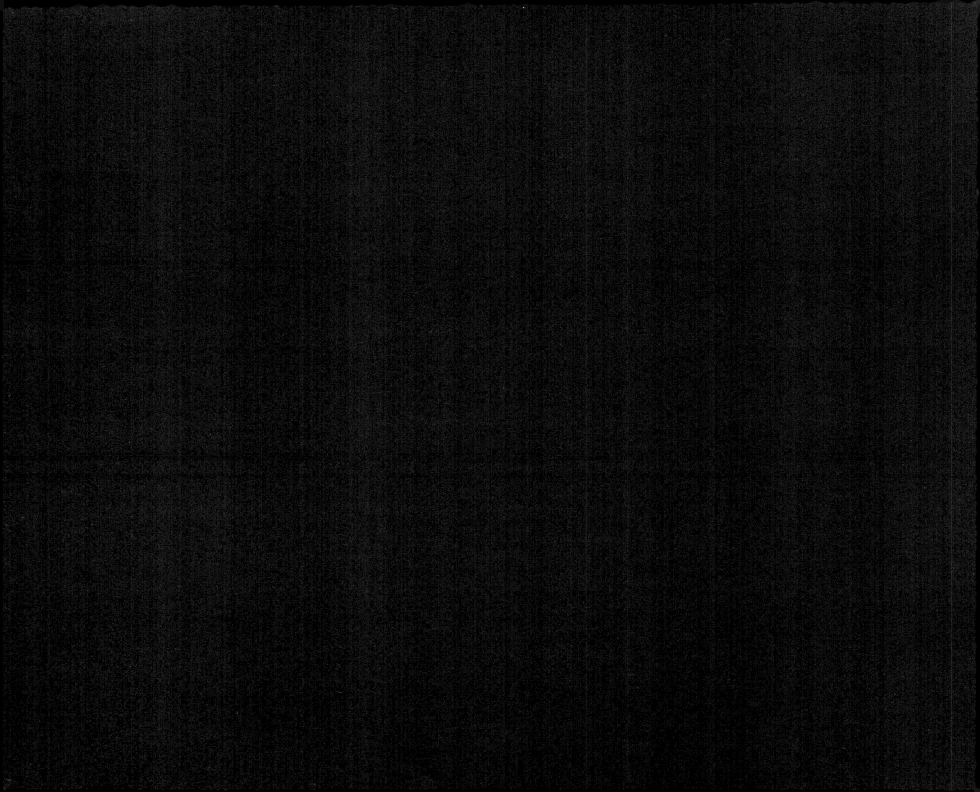

A Vital Activity

Central Market: Cornerstone of the Lancaster Community

❦ A Vital Activity

To enter Central Market on a busy market day is to dive into a heady mix of sights, sounds, and smells. Money and goods change hands across stalls laden with products against the steady hum of conversation. Customers make their way from stand to stand, comparing the price and quality of fruits and vegetables, purchasing milk from a local dairy, buying farm eggs and bread, or deciding on a cut of meat for dinner. Joining them are people grabbing a bite for breakfast or lunch, and tourists soaking up the local atmosphere and purchasing souvenirs.

From the moment one enters Central Market, it is clear that this is a place of essential commerce. This is the environment of a community at work and, sometimes, at play.

Market day. 2009.
PHOTO: MELISSA CARROLL

Opposite page: Mail carrier Greg Smith pauses for lunch and conversation with standholder Omar Hussein. 1999.
PHOTO: RICHARD K. KENT

❧ A source of community wealth

Central Market was chosen in 1995 as one of only 63 "Great American Public Places."

The economic importance of market to Lancaster cannot be overstated. From the earliest days of the settlement, the market was its commercial foundation and was jealously protected by civic leaders. Its position as the cornerstone of the community was established with Lancaster's designation as a market town by King George II, who decreed "that there shall be a clerk of the market for the said borough, who shall have the assize of bread, wine, beer, wood, and all other provisions brought for the use of the said inhabitants." To protect the public's best interests, the city adopted strict rules for selling on market, reflecting the essential nature of an orderly marketplace and fair trade to the community's economic growth. And it was evident again when the city defended the market against the incursion of privately owned markets by building the grand market house that remains the showpiece of downtown Lancaster.

The activity of market-going strengthened the essential connections between Lancaster's urban and rural communities— a role that it continues to play.

Anna Wilson trims a celery stalk at the Hodecker's Celery stand, a fixture at Central Market for multiple generations before it was replaced in 2008 by another celery vendor. 1999.

PHOTO: RICHARD K. KENT

Central Market endures as the county's primary interface between its diverse and defining cultures, from farmers who work the land to city dwellers and suburbanites who support its industries and institutions. Market-going represents the unspoken interplay between social and civic life, the balance of economic needs with the common good, and the interdependency of past and present.

There is no better place to come to understand how market-going creates both economic and social wealth—a public economy as opposed to simple commercial profit. It also explains the community's devotion to the market and why the market is recognized far beyond Lancaster County as an example of what is genuine and relevant about working public markets. Central Market was chosen in 1995 as one of 63 "Great American Public Places." Four years later, documentation of the market's importance to the community became part of the Library of Congress's Local Legacies project.

❦ Hub of commerce

In 1908, *The North American* reported Central Market to be the biggest market in America. The magazine's article observed:

"Beginning about 1 o'clock every market morning, miscellaneous processions of vehicles from various directions clatter and rumble into Lancaster.... By the time the sun rises, more than 1,500 farmers will have arrived, and by 10 o'clock possibly from 10,000 to 12,000

LOCAL IDIOM is filled with expressions that illuminate the community's relationship to Central Market. "Standholders" sell here, not "vendors," referring to the occupants of the original wooden stalls where farmers conducted their business, lined up four to a 12-foot table. In Lancaster one "stands on market" (meaning you sell there), and you still hear the neighborly fare thee well, "I'll see you on market," at the end of many conversations. The phrase is probably a vestige of the German (and Pennsylvania German) prepositional phrase *auf dem Markt*, with *auf* as the equivalent of the English "on," a specific spatial designation that places something in relation to a horizontal surface. It makes "on market" a particularly revealing expression because it retains the idea of Central Market not so much as we see and understand it today—a building that encloses space—but market in its original form, the market *place*, the ground dedicated to buying and selling of food. The expression "on market" folds activity into place; it defines the common ground on which the community was born, and to which it returns every market day.

Shoppers with their market baskets in Penn Square, 1925.

Tuesday, February, 17, 1931

"This evening I bought oranges at Mettfett's just the size and quality that cost 90 cents a dozen 12 months ago, for 30 cents dozen— the poor growers what could be left for them, after shipping, wholesale and retail profit etc. are deducted?"

—John Bowman, entry from his diary

people will have purchased their eatables...

"At 2 o'clock Saturday morning the doors of the Central Market House are opened; at 3 the buyers begin to arrive. At the other markets people go still earlier. By 9 or 10 the markets are over...

"Saturday is the big market day. From outlying towns, people come on trolley cars with great big baskets. From towns five, 10, and 15 miles away, thrifty housewives come; even from Philadelphia many come on Saturdays with great hampers, to [gather] in the week's supply of vegetables. Scores of families of railroad employees living in Philadelphia who enjoy annual passes do their marketing in Lancaster.

"From 4 o'clock in the morning—before the sun illumines the narrow streets about it—until after 9 o'clock, crowds throng the market house. From 500 to 1000 persons flow in a steady stream along the aisles between the stalls at times."[4]

Americans gradually began making more of their food purchases from corner stores and supermarkets—presumably after sunrise. But the role of Central Market as the primary place to shop for food continued for many Lancastrians well into the second half of the twentieth century. Remarkably, in a 1963 study of the Lancaster markets conducted by the City Planning Commission, more than 90 percent of Central Market and Southern Market customers who were interviewed said they used the market weekly and depended almost exclusively on the market for their

A Bountiful Heritage

Agriculture and the selling of farm goods to the public was not only a source of pride for Lancaster County and its core city, it created a local economy that was the community's very lifeblood. The Lancaster Board of Trade stated in 1887:

"It is no idle boast that Lancaster possesses the best supplied and cheapest markets in the country; and this in itself affords advantages for the location here of industrial enterprise, and the engagement of cheaper but better satisfied labor than can be found in any centre of population of corresponding size. This is the nearest mart of those who toil the half-million acres of cultivated soil outlying the city; hither they naturally repair on legal errand or for trade; they deal directly with the consumer, and handle without middlemen the perishable products of the soil, of the dairy and of the slaughter-house."[3]

Curb market on County Courthouse steps, East King Street, 1925.   PHOTO: LANCASTERHISTORY.ORG

"I can tell you how habits and times are changing. In my day there were no malls. The downtown had everything. Starting with early morning farmers market—and I mean early. Tuesday and Friday before daylight the farmers drove their wagons to town. They backed up to the curb along East King Street from the courthouse toward Penn Square, and that was in front of Garvin's store. The horses were unhitched and the men or boys took them to a nearby livery stable while the women put up a table and filled it with eatable produce from the wagons. I can remember walking down Duke Street with my Grandmother in the winter in the dark around 6 a.m. always before breakfast. You had to go and get the nicest things available and that had to be early. Often little boys with express wagons would haul your basket home for a nickel. Soon the street markets had to give way to traffic. After automobiles they weren't practical and they moved inside to one of the five buildings we call market houses…"
—Alma S. Mueller (1905–2002; recorded 1992)

regular food purchases. Only 3 percent of Central Market customers and 4 percent of Southern Market customers said they regularly shopped in suburban shopping centers. At Central Market alone it was estimated that 15,000 people entered the market on a single market day.

Although it is undoubtedly true that a smaller percentage of today's market-goers buy the majority of their food at Central Market, a survey of shoppers taken in 2001 found that nearly half of respondents (46 percent) said the reason they came to market was to buy groceries. Moreover, 43 percent of the shoppers surveyed stated that they most typically bought produce—compared to 28 percent for baked goods and 25 percent for meats—and many said the availability of locally grown produce was important to them.[5] Another survey, conducted in 2004 as part of the process for creating a master plan for the market, found that 70 percent of shoppers purchased produce at market and half bought baked goods.[6] These findings clearly support the idea that despite the changing character of the modern market, its primary purpose in the minds of its patrons remains that of a place to purchase fresh foods.

❦ Balancing the mix

One of the biggest challenges facing Central Market in the twenty-first century lies in defining its identity and economic role, the activities that take place there. Is it a farmers market? A tourist attraction? A food court? Elements of all of these are visible on any given market day.

If it weren't for our farmers,

What markets would be had?

We wouldn't have a thing to eat

And wouldn't that be bad!

Wann's net fer unsere Bauere waer,

Was waer dann unser Marrick?

Mer hett yoh nix zu fresse meh—

Un sell waer drumm so arrick!

—Old German song

PHOTO: MARJORY COLLINS, NOVEMBER, 1942.

LIBRARY OF CONGRESS, PRINTS & PHOTOGRAPHS DIVISION,

FSA-OWI COLLECTION, LCUSW3-011007-E

A standholder's simple message provides evidence of the spiritual beliefs that are part of Lancaster County's Amish and Mennonite heritage. 1999.

PHOTO: RICHARD K. KENT

Yet Central Market's purpose first and foremost as a home for Lancaster's farmers and their products is what has sustained it from its beginnings. This is what has shaped, for nearly 300 years, the patterns of local life in Lancaster as a market town. Such authenticity is rare; it distinguishes Central Market from the manufactured retail experiences of contemporary life and enables it to survive as other public markets succumbed to modern economic pressures.

The struggle to retain the market's character has been hard-fought. Lancaster citizens publicly registered their unease about Central Market's changing face starting in the 1960s. In 1963, as America's farmers markets were all but extinguished by suburban retailing, the City Planning Commission issued its study of Central Market, recommending ways of modernizing and improving it. A December 28, 1965, editorial in the *Lancaster New Era* urged the city to maintain the character of the market, fearing that farmers would be crowded out by vendors selling knick-knacks and tourist novelties. A subsequent article written about a month later mirrored this worry, questioning whether the market should be "plain or fancy"—referring to the introduction of stands "dressed up" with high backs and rooflines. Anxiety resurfaced in the late 1980s with the increasing number of prepared-food stands and the loss of small-farm stands.

In March 2005, the master plan commissioned by Lancaster City, Lancaster County, and the Lancaster Chamber of Commerce and Industry addressed the future of the market. The document contained a wide range of findings and recommendations. It notes, "There is widespread consensus in the community that Central Market should continue to function as a source of fresh food, a strategic economic element of downtown and a place where all Lancastrians and visitors can meet and interact. While so many public spaces now are filled with the 'absent presence' of individuals listening to music or talking on cell phones, the Central Market, by definition, encourages people to take part in an activity with others."

For Lancaster, there is much at stake in the ability to protect Central Market's fragile cultural character. The market has already shown itself to be vulnerable to downtown development, loss of farmland, and the import of foods from all over the globe. Planning for its life in the twenty-first century will be a critical test. As the master plan notes, "The challenge for market management will be to safeguard the interests of market customers and standholders throughout, and to ensure the changes bring in more shoppers, address customer needs, result in more business for Central Market standholders, and keep the public purpose of Central Market."

Nearly one million acres of Lancaster's farmland, the world's most fertile soil, has been paved over in the last fifty years. Between 1984 and 1999 the number of all local growers occupying stalls at Central Market dropped from twenty-two to eight.

"LANCASTER FARM" IMAGE: LANCASTERHISTORY.ORG

❦ Operating the market

City-run markets were once icons of the greatness of urban America and municipal government. Public markets, strictly controlled by municipal authorities, helped protect citizens from entrepreneurs who bought and hoarded food stores, artificially driving up prices, or who sold contaminated food. Well-regulated public markets were the pride of towns and the palpable measure of the quality of local government, a fact understood from the symbolism of their central location and proximity to town halls, courthouses, and jails.

Throughout most of the nineteenth and twentieth centuries, Central Market was supervised by a committee made up of elected members of the Select and Common Councils of Lancaster, the latter representing the city's wards. These men were responsible for determining the rules and regulations of the market, which were brought before the full body of councilmen where they were publicly, often loudly, debated. The day-to-day market was the responsibility of the market master, a member of Lancaster's constabulary.

In 1945, a comprehensive municipal plan developed by the engineer Michael Baker moved oversight of the Bureau of Markets to the city's Department of Public Works. Fifty years later, at the recommendation of the Central Market Master Plan, a non-profit entity was created to manage the city-owned market more actively and with greater attention to the business strategies that will secure its future. That entity is the

The trusses that support the market house's vast roof are one of the structure's most distinctive and impressive features.

PHOTO: RICHARD K. KENT

Central Market Trust, established July 1, 2005 and charged with:

— Ensuring that Central Market has the vision, overall decision-making structure, day-to-day management focus, and resources it needs to be an economically successful and financially stable market over the long term;

— Maintaining, preserving and interpreting the historic Central Market House as a unique community asset; and

— Maintaining Central Market's civic role within an ever-changing context.

In its initial years of operation, the Trust posted significant progress on many fronts. It established new product mix guidelines, adopted new operating rules and entered into new lease agreements with standholders. Perhaps most significantly, it initiated a $7 million capital improvement plan to upgrade the market's mechanical systems and perform maintenance on the market house that had been neglected for many years.

Former market master Don Horn takes time out from his paperwork to entertain his grandson at his desk on the market mezzanine. 1999.

PHOTO: RICHARD K. KENT

Curbside Selling: Lancaster Markets At Their Height

When public selling by family farmers was the predominant means by which people filled their pantries, Lancaster's market was too big to be contained within the center square. It spilled out of the market house and into the surrounding streets and alleys, filling the downtown with carts, horses, food, and farmers.

Curb market along South Queen Street, 1926.

PHOTO: LANCASTERHISTORY.ORG

Curbside Selling: Lancaster Markets At Their Height

Central Market: Cornerstone of the Lancaster Community

Although "curbstone" selling of food had been an auxiliary to Central Market since the 1700s, by 1820 it was formalized and regulated through city ordinance. In 1818 the curb markets lined the Centre Square (today's Penn Square) and West King Street to Prince Street. By 1845 they extended a block both north and south along Queen Street, and by 1898 encroached onto East King and Duke Streets. At their height, the curb markets filled East King Street to Duke Street, seeping into the alley behind the Courthouse (now named Lennox Alley after one of the main produce vendors who sold there), continued down Duke Street to Vine Street, ran along the Southern Market from Vine Street to Prince Street, then north to Orange Street. These curb markets were commemorated in a famous set of photographs as well as in postcard sets and an unpublished sequence of snapshots

The curbside market along South Queen Street, 1926.

PHOTO: LANCASTERHISTORY.ORG

Opposite page: Farmers lined up their buggies and wagons along East King Street and set up tables on the sidewalks, circa 1910.

PHOTO: LANCASTERHISTORY.ORG

Curbside Selling: Lancaster Markets At Their Height

taken in 1926 from the upper story of the former Conestoga Bank on Center Square. Although no known photographs exist showing the activity of the old market before the middle of the nineteenth century, the images of the curb markets provide an indication of how the early central marketplace might have appeared.

Despite their regulation, the curb markets were important sources of income for non-farming as well as farm families. Lavina Stephens was 83 when she recalled in a 1997 interview how she would help her mother load two baskets of produce from their family garden in Neffsville. Together they rode the trolley into Lancaster where her mother stood and sold on King Street.

The curb markets also became the conduit that brought farmers into the newly built Central Market house. Registered curbsellers were offered places inside the Central Market, and several of the original Central Market standholder families moved into the market from streetside.

The curbside market along South Queen Street, 1926.

PHOTO: LANCASTERHISTORY.ORG

Opposite page: The curb market on South Duke Street, circa 1920s.

PHOTO: LANCASTERHISTORY.ORG

Curbside Selling: Lancaster Markets At Their Height

A view of the curb market along the first block of East King Street.

Curbside Selling: Lancaster Markets At Their Height

"On East King Street the carriages were backed up on East King and the farmers had their

vegetables and everything that they brought in to sell right there along the curb. Those horses

were stabled also on Howard Avenue, and also on East King Street on the south side, there

was a stable in the middle of the block. It later became a garage."

—Lillian Rote Martin (1906–1996; recorded 1992)

The Community of Market

🌿 The Community of Market

"I first came to the market as a single person who had just moved to Lancaster. Later, I came pushing strollers and wearing backpacks with babies through the aisles. Now my children are all grown but they still ask to come to the market when they come home to visit with their new spouses. Hopefully someday I'll be able to bring my grandchildren."

Above: A busy market day, sometime between 1966 and 1973.
PHOTO: LANCASTERHISTORY.ORG

What does it mean to be part of a market community? Central Market can have the effect of rooting us so firmly that we believe our experience is the experience of all of Lancaster. But Central Market, like Lancaster, is a living place; its character shifts and changes—sometimes we recognize it, other times it challenges us to navigate the realities of an increasingly diverse, modern city.

Opposite page: John Stoner, standing next to his wife, Ethel, is the third generation of his family to have a stand on market. 1999.
PHOTO: RICHARD K. KENT

'A better place to be'

The qualities that make Central Market essential to community life in Lancaster are bred in its bones. Several present-day standholder families, many descended from the Plain Sects for which Lancaster County is well known, have sold "on market" for multiple generations— and many current-day patrons can say the same about the generations of their families that have shopped there. Although the number of multi-generational standholders is decreasing, those who remain are a testament to the stability that gives life on the market floor its rhythm. Such stability creates a sense of community that is intensely social by virtue of the mutual dedication of its members to each other and their collective dedication to

Standholders try hard to meet the needs

of individual customers by maintaining

an attitude of, 'If I don't have it now,

I will get it for you soon.'

Pickle and hot pepper stand, 1997.

the people who shop there. Ethel Stoner of John R. Stoner's Vegetable Farm, which represents the third generation of Stoners on market, explained in a 1999 interview:

"One thing that is so important is the personal relationship you develop with customers. And the ability to care for their individual tastes. Market is a place to meet all kinds of people. One gets to know them and their families, and many friendships develop. John [Stoner] tries hard to meet individual needs of customers, the 'if I don't have it now, I will get it for you soon' attitude. What also makes the market unique is that many of the standholders like us have planned and planted and harvested [and] prepared their product themselves and now are bringing that product to sell to the customers themselves. That makes for a quality that cannot be found anywhere else."

Busy aisles, 2008.

PHOTO: MELISSA CARROLL

The Community of Market

Simple exchanges of courtesy and familiarity are the bedrock of market relations and create the social texture of a market day. Even after many years of retirement, Charlie Long of Long's Famous Horseradish continued to visit market to see old customers. "Every time somebody comes up, 'Didn't see you for awhile,' they say, 'You still around? You still in business?' They use my name, 'Mr. Horseradish'!" chortled Long, whose son Michael carries on the family tradition. Another standholder, Jim Zink of The Herb Shop, said, "I don't know how to explain it. [As a standholder] you don't make a lot of money here. It's hard work. But it's a better place to be. Qualitatively, it's just a better life."

Jim Zink, The Herb Shop, 2008.

PHOTO: MELISSA CARROLL

Opposite page: Michael Long, right, is the fourth generation to sell freshly made horseradish at Central Market, providing one of the market's most-memorable aromas. His father, Charlie, left, operated the stand for many years before retiring. 1999.

PHOTO: RICHARD K. KENT

IT'S A TUESDAY MORNING IN 2007, and early-bird market-goers are arriving to a puzzling scene. The market is dark. The refrigerated cases are silent. The mood is somber. The building's aging electrical system has given out, and although it will be fixed the next day, the experience of seeing the market go dark has a profound impact on that morning's patrons. "For a moment," one of them recounts, "I realized how much poorer our community would be... how much poorer my life would be if our Central Market shut down. I know I wasn't the only person to realize just what a community treasure this really is. The only light moment of the morning was when someone asked a young Amish woman tending a stand where her lanterns were!"

❦ Family ties

It's difficult to fully capture the immensity of time and feeling that Central Market holds in human memories and communal history. Many of the recollections of Lancaster's markets are deeply personal. Standholders and customers alike characterize Central Market's longevity and endurance specifically in terms of their family history. This isn't surprising, given that going to market was historically a family occasion both for standholders and customers—and remains so to this day. Standholders are justifiably proud that they have handed down the family business for generations.

"I worked at it until I was seventy years or seventy-two, I guess. I finally gave the business to my son Mike here, and he took it over," Charlie Long explained. "I was at the Market for fifty-five years…and he's got a big business now. So it's a carry-on, in other words. If his sons take it, it'll be the fifth generation. It's the oldest stand here as far as being the same place, the same time [all the time] and it's the only stand that's the original. By that I mean the original owners carried down."

In what was a fairly common occurrence, the families of Mary Breighner and the late Myrtle Howry Funk sold curbside before the construction of the present Central Market house. Mrs. Breighner, who left market after nearly seventy years selling there, recalled that her grandfather was one of the original standholders to go inside the new

Going to market was historically a family occasion both for standholders and customers— and it remains so to this day.

Opposite page: Before leaving market in the first decade of the twenty-first century, Mary Breighner represented Central Market's oldest standholder family, stretching back to the 1880s. 1999.
PHOTO: RICHARD K. KENT

Central Market: Cornerstone of the Lancaster Community

building from the curb market. Likewise, Mrs. Funk's father, Edward Aaron Howry, first of a long line of Howry butchers to attend the market, operated a stand on the old curb market before he moved into the new Central Market house. As was the custom in those days, he dressed and sold meats only during the fall, winter and spring. During the summer months he sold his strawberries and other fruits and vegetables.

The Stoner family has a similar heritage. Ethel Stoner remarked, "We are not sure if [John's] grandfather was part of the curb market. His father had been selling cars in the forties when World War II came along and left that job to start farming and attending market during that time. He remained at the market and John joined him when he was out of high school. John remembers the days when he thought he would be making a lot of money if he got 25 cents for his things. He was charging only 15 cents for things like a box of turnips or potatoes, and so 25 cents looked like big money."

With only a handful of old market families remaining, such connections to the past are more fragile than ever. But the fact that they exist at all reflects their continuing importance to the market's survival.

Wendy Jo's Homemade in Central Market, 2008.

PHOTO: MELISSA CARROLL

Opposite page: Tender, curving stalks of homegrown celery, a Central Market standard, are a stark contrast to the bright green, ramrod straight celery found in supermarkets. 1999.

PHOTO: RICHARD K. KENT

Florist Viv Hunt holds a photograph taken of her mother, Mabel Haverstick, behind the family stand. Her stand has since been turned over to another flower vendor. 1999.

PHOTO: RICHARD K. KENT

🌸 An evolving community

"My greatest fondness has always been the people on the market, not necessarily the customers but the other standholders, even as a kid. On the Southern Market across from us there were two ladies that were never married and they had homegrown produce and flowers and they were the sweetest ladies… Even now coming in I couldn't think of a more fun place to work… you're always doing something and there are people to talk to… It's really what I like about market… People will stop and talk to me, you get to learn their names…a couple at a time…people come up and say 'good morning' [to you by name] and it's nice."

—Michael Long, Long's Famous Horseradish

Central Market shoppers echo the love of market expressed by long-time standholders. When, as part of a comprehensive planning process in the early 1990s, several hundred Lancastrians were asked what they liked best about the city, the predominant response was Central Market. Why? Because market is a place to buy a variety of high-quality food products at reasonable prices. Because shopping at market is a unique, historic and satisfying experience. But perhaps most of all, because market is an opportunity to continually reconnect with the community.

Without question, the multi-generation standholders and shoppers at Central Market provide the continuity and stability that is at least partly responsible for its endurance. At the same time, however, newcomers to

Continued on page 61

A mother

walking up

Market Street with her daughter

greeted a friend with a big smile and

exclaimed, "You're number one!"

Seeing the friend's bemused look, she

added, "You're the first person we've

seen who we know. We have a bet

on how many there will be!"

PHOTO: MARJORY COLLINS, NOVEMBER, 1942.

LIBRARY OF CONGRESS, PRINTS & PHOTOGRAPHS DIVISION,

FSA-OWI COLLECTION, LCUSW3-010944-E,

❧ *Children speak about the Market*

In 2005, seventh and eighth graders from The New School of Lancaster spent a semester visiting the market, observing it and writing poems that are wry and insightful.

"Dried Flower Cowboy"
Katie Herzog

Only in the melting pot that is Central Market
can you find a Quarryville cowboy
who has the confidence of an old-time veteran
but is really a relative newcomer.
This cowboy from Quarryville can fool a lot of people.
He describes the patterns of Market customers
    with confidence;
the new customers wander around taking
    everything in
but the regulars know exactly what they want and
    where to get it.
Simple. Right?

Only Market is not so simple.
Community is strong and history is rich.
Inside one building lives a culture like no other.
Trust is the basis and family is the result.
Whether you want dried sunflowers or seafood,
    coffee or horseradish
there is a stand holder who would be glad to see you.
Diversity is what holds Market together
and there is no shortage of it,
but no mixture is complete
    without a little southern flair
and a few dried flowers.

"Latino Comida de Reina" (2005)

A poem by David Bishop, seventh-grader at The New School.

Arroz blanco, arroz Amarillo,

empanadas de

pollo y carne de res,

arroz gardules,

son deliciosos los duraznos.

Los dueños de los otros dioskos son agradables,

la gente que viene también.

Una sociologista

jubilada, pero trabahando como le gusta.

El major y único sitio donde se quede

encontrar comida Puerto Riqueña,

en el Mercado.

Para saborear lo que quiere.

Sin embargo, la clientela

no es Puerto Riqueña,

este sitio es más popular

con las personas que no son de ese país.

Un Nuevo toque añadido

al Mercado.

Algo diferente, unico.

Un trabajo ardueo,

pero satisfactorio.

"Reina's Latino Mix" (2005)

White rice, yellow rice,

chicken and beef

empanadas,

rice gardules,

peaches are good.

The other stand-holders are nice,

the people that come too.

A sociologist,

retired, but working as she likes.

The best and only place where one can

find Puerto Rican food

in the market.

To taste what you want.

The clientele

is not Puerto Rican, however,

this place is more popular with those

not from there.

A new touch added

to the market,

something different, unique.

Hard work,

but satisfying.

Members of the Amish community continue to be a part of Central Market's tapestry of cultures. Here, Lydia Smoker sells bulk foods. 1999.

PHOTO: RICHARD K. KENT

Continued from page 57

Lancaster and new trends in society constantly refresh, energize and challenge the market to maintain its relevance in today's world. Some signs of this are found in the foods at market. Ethnic cuisines, organic foods and heirloom produce are increasingly visible in the modern market for example, reflecting the growing diversity of peoples in the city and county. Central Market's international mix of buyers and sellers at times seems unlikely. The person behind the stand might be a native of Uganda or Bird-in-Hand, of the Middle East or Quarryville, of Puerto Rico or Manheim Township. The person buying from them might be a city resident in search of local farm products, a county native drawn by the selection of ethnic foods, or a recent transplant from the Midwest.

One measure of a public market is its ability to create a place that includes people from all walks of life, of diverse ethnic and racial backgrounds, and the full spectrum of social and economic status. In principle, public markets were intended to be this common ground on which all types of people come together as equals. Bellwethers of civic health, such places are essential to the social and, indeed, economic success of any city, anywhere.

Mabel Haverstick at her stand in Central Market, circa 1950s–60s.

PHOTO: COURTESY VIVIAN HUNT

❧ *Central Market's Plain Community*

By foundation, Central Market is a public, civic, commercial space. But its distinctive character has flowered from the intrinsically agrarian values of Lancaster's Plain Sects and their deep roots in the region.

Above and at right: Standholders, 1942.

PHOTO: MARJORY COLLINS, NOVEMBER, 1942.

LIBRARY OF CONGRESS, PRINTS & PHOTOGRAPHS DIVISION,

FSA-OWI COLLECTION, LCUSW3-011009-E

AND LCUSW3-011035-E

Inherent to the identity of Lancaster's traditional farming community, which has helped provision the market for all of its existence, is a belief in "the gift of good land" and the spiritual significance of the soil as a remnant of the Garden of Eden. Farmland is to be tended, protected, and used as the basis for community life, both for the human sustenance it yields and as a sign of God's vision for His children.[7] With good management, land will not only yield a livelihood, it should reflect the qualities of pleasantness and order.

The sacred and secular meld together in Lancaster's market, not simply because of the visible presence of the Amish and Mennonites who work there. At market, the indulgence of the senses and worldly appetites are punctuated with moments of greater restraint. Here food can be seen as a gift of the soil and of God's grace; the abundance of that gift is reflected not in quantity alone, but in the orderly rows of exquisite produce, carefully hand-selected and laid out on the stands.

Opposite page: Locally grown produce, such as these offerings at the Rohrer Groff stand, is a Central Market favorite. 1999.
PHOTO: RICHARD K. KENT

Central Market: Cornerstone of the Lancaster Community

The Community of Market

🌿 A Sense of belonging:
Voices from the Oral History Project

For nearly ten years, The Friends of Central Market has been conducting an Oral History Project to document the aspects of market that make it a special place for those who shop and sell there. One of the most striking themes to emerge from the project has been the degree to which the sense of belonging in Lancaster—and to Lancaster—is nurtured week after week at market. Long-time residents and newcomers alike feel themselves linked over time and bonded to a community. Here are some of their voices, all from 1998:

"As a child of the 1930s, I remember my mother bringing me to Central Market on Tuesdays. It was an all-day affair, driving from Kaolin (near Avondale) [in Chester County] and we'd stop off at auctions along the way, whenever available. I recall gorging on donuts and taking home wonderful Lebanon bologna, cheeses, other meats, chocolate éclairs — always a marvelous day — still remembered by me as I have lived in Kentucky the past 49 years — Thank you all!"

🌿

"My grandmother and mother both worked at Pfannebecker's Bakery Stand. I grew up coming to market with my parents. Lancaster had many markets, Southern, West End, Fulton, Central, and Arcade. Market is deep in my roots. My children also came to market before going to work on Tuesdays and Fridays. Thank you for keeping market going."

🌿

"I've lived in Lancaster County for the past thirteen years. It has only been within the last four years that I have 'discovered' the market experience. Every Saturday morning I look forward to a nice cup of coffee, a long john donut, and a lemon poppy muffin. This is not to mention the other wonderful tastes and treats that market has to offer. Visiting market has become an important part of my life. I find something new to enjoy every week."

❦

"When I was young, my grandmother… used to babysit me, and every Friday her daughter (my aunt)… would pick us up and we'd all come to the market. As we perused all the stands, making occasional purchases, our family bonds were formed. Through the years, and after the death of my grandmother, my fondest recollections are the ones of those Friday afternoons spent with my grandmother and aunt at the market."

❦

A shopper at the East King Street curb market.

PHOTO: LANCASTERHISTORY.ORG

"My grandmother (mam mam), my aunt and I would get together on a Friday. We would first go to market, shopping at our favorite stands. It was and is a treat to come to market. Now, on occasion, my sister and I come to market to buy our favorite things, which were developed long ago. When we have family visiting from out of state, we always take them to Central Market. You usually end up seeing an old acquaintance you haven't seen for some time. Market is the essence of Lancaster."

❦

Central Market standholder, 1942.

"My earliest memories of 'market' are of coming there as a kid with my mom and sister. We got the bus from Rohrerstown and rode in to the square, where the bus bounced over the trolley tracks that circled the monument.

"At that time, market gave me a sense of how small I was. The stands and all the people towered over me. I gained some stature when my mom would let me stand on the seat-type benches that extend in front of the stalls…

"Today, we still come to market, and our children, Matt and Jenny, do, too, occasionally, when they're in town. Things have changed. Most of the meat stands have gone, although the lady that called all her female customers 'misses' is still there. Shad roe isn't quite the same if you can't get it from Stetters (in the rear).

"Basically market remains, and we love it. The smells are the best thing. The mix of meat and cheese odors from Weaver's is worth the trip, and the standholders greet us 'regular customers' like old friends."

Central Market: Cornerstone of the Lancaster Community

❦ The Friends of Central Market

Formed in 1997, The Friends of Central Market is a non-profit organization that serves as a steward and an advocate on behalf of the market's public functions and historic architecture. The first grassroots effort to describe a vision of the market as Lancaster's premier center for locally grown and produced foods, The Friends of Central Market is also the first organization created by citizens that is devoted to raising awareness of the importance of the market to the identity and community well-being of Lancaster. The organization accomplishes that objective in several ways. It increases awareness of the market through activities and outreach. It helps manage the Lancaster Buy Fresh Buy Local® campaign and promotes local farm products in the market. It supports preservation initiatives on behalf of the historic market house. And it creates a foundation for the commercial success of Central Market by providing experience, energy, and ideas to assist the Central Market Trust.

In addition to sponsoring events such as Harvest Breakfast and Hot Spiced Saturday, The Friends of Central Market has been deeply involved in developing original research that contributes to a better understanding of the market's contribution to the community—both historically and in modern times—and to the proper stewardship of the market house. The organization spearheaded "Central Market in our Community Food System," a report published in 2004 on Central Market's role in Lancaster's urban food system. The project was undertaken in association with The Center for Liberal Arts and Society and The Center for the Study of Local Economy at Franklin and Marshall College. In addition, The Friends of Central Market commissioned a preservation planning report for Central Market, published in 2009, that includes the first exhaustive architectural examination of the market house and provides recommendations for its preservation and development, as well as design recommendations that will help guide future work on the market house and protect the architectural and historical integrity of building and site.

In 2007, The Friends of Central Market was awarded a Special Recognition Award for Smart Growth Leadership by the Lancaster County Planning Commission, for managing the Buy Fresh Buy Local campaign and for its work promoting local foods and farms.

❦

Afterword

Afterword

"The Market's Future Awaits our Discovery of the Past..."

—EDITORIAL HEADLINE, LANCASTER *INTELLIGENCER JOURNAL*, DECEMBER 31, 1973.

No one can know what the future holds for Central Market, just as no one in the 1730s could have imagined what Lancaster's Central Market would become. Market-goers of the late nineteenth and early twentieth centuries shopped amid hundreds of farm stalls sprawling for blocks throughout downtown; would they find today's market to be only a ghost of its former self? Shoppers of the twenty-first century live in a retail world dominated by superstores, where food is routinely transported thousands of miles; will they marvel that Central Market remains a viable institution in the marketplace that nineteenth century city fathers so ardently fought to defend?

The net effect of current economic, social, and political forces on Central Market remains to be seen. Without question, the past several decades have tested the community's commitment to Central Market. Food shopping patterns have changed dramatically, Lancaster farmland has rapidly disappeared beneath housing developments and shopping

Opposite page: Farmer Earl Groff, known for his naturally grown produce, is a familiar face to Central Market regulars. 1999.

PHOTO: RICHARD K. KENT

71

Central Market standholder, 1942.

malls, and the number of working farmers who sell their own products on market has steadily declined.

Still, there are reasons for genuine optimism as the first decade of the twenty-first century draws to a close. Paradoxically, the survival of Central Market for three centuries has made it more relevant than ever. A growing recognition that the world's fossil fuel based economy is unsustainable has prompted many consumers to purchase locally produced food and support local farmers, whose products traverse the county, not the hemisphere. Central Market provides an ideal venue for supporting this commitment. Downtown Lancaster itself is experiencing a resurgence as more people reinvest in urban life, seeking ways to reconnect to real places and to each other. Residents and visitors alike are drawn into the city center where many are introduced, or reintroduced, to the unique qualities of Central Market.

Ultimately, we all are creating the future of Central Market. The Central Market Trust is dedicated to helping the market respond more ably to its many challenges: preserving the essential ties to local agriculture, increasing the ethnic and social diversity both of shoppers and standholders, and ensuring that the market remains the bedrock of a community of diverse, sometimes challenging needs. The existence of an

Central Market: Cornerstone of the Lancaster Community

active market advocacy group, The Friends of Central Market, equally reflects the depth of the community's devotion to the market. Through the Central Market Campaign, many donors have clearly demonstrated their love for the market by contributing generously toward its much-needed repairs and upgrades. Those who have continued to shop steadfastly and without fanfare at Central Market also make their contribution.

The sum of these acts, large and small, are reminders that the spirit of market and community are intertwined, the result of an intentional collaboration among us all.

Central Market standholder, 1942.

PHOTO: MARJORY COLLINS, NOVEMBER, 1942.

LIBRARY OF CONGRESS, PRINTS & PHOTOGRAPHS DIVISION,

FSA-OWI COLLECTION, LCUSW3-011012-E

Appendix I: Resources

Aleci, Eugene. "Story of a Building Project," *Slow*, no. 46 (2004): 54–59.

Aleci, Linda. *Central Market and the Tradition of Market in Lancaster County*, manuscript on deposit, Library of Congress, Archives of American Folklife, 1999.

Aleci, Linda, principal author. *Central Market in our Community Food System*. Local Economy Center, Working Paper 1 (2004).

Aleci, Linda. "On Market," *Slow*, no. 46 (2004): 50–53.

Barshinger, Jay. "Provisions for Trade: The Market House in Southeastern Pennsylvania." Unpublished doctoral dissertation, Pennsylvania State University, 1995.

Baer, Meryl. "The Central Market: A Colonial Legacy." Unpublished Masters' Thesis, The Pennsylvania State University, 1975.

Ducker, Dan. "History of Lancaster's Central Market," *Susquehanna*, 8, no. 11 (November 1983): 19–25.

Heisey, M. Luther. "The Famed Markets of Lancaster," *Papers of the Lancaster County Historical Society*, 53 (1949): 1–31.

Hostetler, John A. *Amish Roots.* Baltimore, 1989.

Lancaster Central Market: Assessments, Guidelines, &
Recommendations for Preservation and Development.
Prepared by Linda S. Aleci, Community Heritage Partners,
Paden de la Fuente Architects, and Hammel Associates
Architects, LLC, for The Friends of Central Market, 2009.

Lancaster Central Market Master Plan: Resource Book. Prepared by
Murphy & Dittenhafer Architects, 2005.

Mayo, James M. "The American Public Market," *Journal of*
Architectural Education, 45, n. 1 (1991), pp. 41–57.

Schmiechen, James, and Kenneth Carls, *The British Market Hall.*
A Social and Architectural History. New Haven, 1999.

Schneider, David B., and Heidi M. Pawlowski, *Historic Farming*
Resources of Lancaster County. Historic Preservation Trust
of Lancaster County, Rural Preservation Project, 1994.

Tangires, Helen. *Public Markets.* Norton/Library of Congress Visual
Sourcebooks in Architecture, Design and Engineering, 2008.

Tangires, Helen. *Public Markets and Civic Culture in Nineteenth-*
Century America. Baltimore, 2003.

Tangires, Helen. "The Country Connection: Farmers' Markets in the
    Public Eye," *Pennsylvania Heritage* 24, no. 4 (Fall 1998): 4–11.

The Friends of Central Market Oral History Project and Project Diary,
    1997 to present.

Weaver, William Woys. "Sauerkraut Yankees." *Pennsylvania-German
    Foods and Foodways*. Philadelphia, 1983.

Appendix II: Central Market Timeline

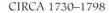

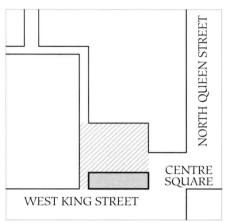

May 16, 1730—Andrew Hamilton and his wife, Ann, convey from their private estate a 120-square-foot lot in the northwest corner of the intersection the King's Highway (today's King Street) and Lancaster's main north-south road (today's Queen Street) for use as a public market.

1742   King George II of England formally charters the borough and conveys to it the coveted designation of a market town. Shortly after receiving the market town designation, the market clerk erects six permanent stalls, eight feet by five feet each—the first market stalls.

1752   First known reference to a permanent "market house" in borough records. Stalls rented for seven shillings apiece.

1757   Lancaster's Burgesses authorize the erection of a market building, likely a rudimentary structure consisting of rows of stalls covered with a roof, later redone in oak shingles and the floor paved in brick.

1773   Market house roof reshingled in oak.

1775   Market Square paved.

1790   Temporary shed addition built "for the benefit of the country people."

1795   Construction of county offices (later City Hall) begins at southeast corner of Market Square.

CIRCA 1798–1854

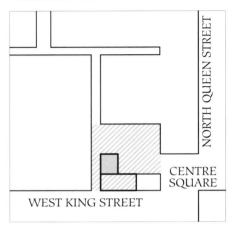

CIRCA 1854–1876

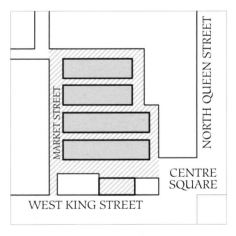

1798   Freemason Lodge #43 constructs their meetinghouse in Market Square. It sits above an open arcade built jointly by the town and the masons to house twenty-four market stalls.

1818   Lancaster is incorporated as a city. The specific duties of the clerk of the market are established by city ordinance. In addition to checking weights and measures, "weigh[ing], try[ing], and examin[ing] all butter, lard, and other articles of provision," he is required to attend market during market hours, "and open the same by ringing the bell," collect stall rents and see to the cleanliness of the market house.

1853   Second courthouse in Centre Square is demolished.

1854   City purchases and clears six properties adjacent to Market Square, expanding 44 feet west and 125 feet north. Union Court alley is vacated and a new Market Street opens on the western side of the square. Four parallel market sheds fill the new square and market activities continue under the arcade.

1856   New commercial structures built adjacent to the Masonic Lodge at the southwest corner of Market Square.

1870   The position of market master is created to replace the clerk of market. All financial and administrative responsibilities are passed to the city treasurer and the market master becomes supervisor of all operations of the market "on the floor."

1872   Lancaster's first private market house, Farmers Northern Market, opens three blocks north at Queen and Walnut Streets.

1876   Market sheds are improved and enclosed into two larger sheds.

1883   Farmers Eastern Market opens three blocks east at King and Shippen Streets followed later in the year by Farmers Western Market, five blocks west at Orange and Pine Streets.

1888   Farmers Southern Market opens one block south at Queen and Vine Streets.

1889   Lancaster builds a new municipal market house, designed by English architect James Warner to rival the private markets. It houses Central Market to this day.

1925   Restaurant opens in southeast tower, replacing original restroom.

1927   Lancaster's curb markets are outlawed, in a concession to the growing number of automobiles in the city. The city leases the Southern Farmers Market in order to accommodate the displaced farmers.

1960   Original slate roof replaced with asphalt shingles.

1972   Central Market is placed on the National Register of Historic Places.

1973   Central Market undergoes significant modifications with the addition of large sconce lights at the doorways, the elimination of the cart ways and curbs, and the placement of bollards around the perimeter of the building to make a combined vehicular and pedestrian area.

1974   Extensive interior alterations.

1985   Southern Market closes, leaving Central Market as the only remaining municipal market in Lancaster.

1995   Central Market is chosen as one of 63 "Great American Public Places" as part of an initiative sponsored by the Lyndhurst Foundation of

CIRCA 1876–1889

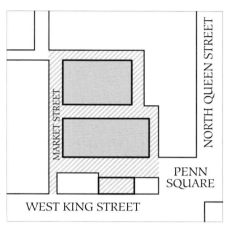

CIRCA 1899–PRESENT

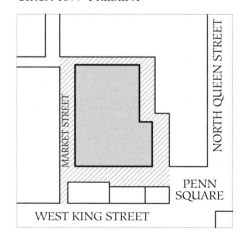

Chattanooga, Tennessee.

1997   The Friends of Central Market is founded as a non-profit organization serving as a steward of the public market. Its primary mission is to protect and support the Central Market as Lancaster's primary source for locally grown and produced farm products and to protect the integrity of the historic market house and its site.

2000   Central Market is designated a Local Legacy by the Library of Congress.

2004   The Friends of Central Market publishes "Central Market in our Community Food System," a report on the role of the market in Lancaster's urban food system.

2005   The City of Lancaster completes the Central Market Master Plan.

2006   Central Market Trust, a non-profit organization, is created to oversee the management of the market. The city retains ownership of the property.

2009   The Friends of Central Market issues a preservation plan entitled "Lancaster Central Market: Assessments, Guidelines & Recommendations for Preservation and Development."

2009   Central Market Trust concludes a $7 million capital campaign to fund essential upgrades to the market's utility systems as well as structural repairs and streetscape improvements.

Endnotes

1   *The Pictorial Sketchbook of Pennsylvania* (Philadelphia: William Bromwell, 1853), p. 31.

2   *Mrs. Royall's Pennsylvania, or Travels continued in the United States* (Washington [D.C.]: Printed for the author, 1829).

3   *Resources and Industries of the City of Lancaster* (Lancaster, Pa. ["Intelligencer" Printing Establishment] 1887): 27–28.

4   *The North American,* Sunday July 5, 1908.

5   The survey was conducted as part of a study entitled *Central Market in our Community Food System,* a collaborative research project of The Friends of Central Market, Innovation Focus Inc., The Center for Liberal Arts & Society and The Center for the Study of Local Economy, Franklin & Marshal College.

6   *Lancaster Central Market Master Plan,* March 2005.

7   John A. Hostetler, *Amish Roots* (Baltimore: Johns Hopkins University Press, 1989), pp. 5–6; Wendell Berry, *The Gift of Good Land. Further Essays Cultural and Agricultural* (San Francisco: North Point Press, 1981).

Contributors

LINDA ALECI, Ph.D., is a professor at Franklin & Marshall College and is affiliated with the Local Economy Center, Franklin & Marshall College. Trained as an historian, much of her scholarship over the past fifteen years has focused on Central Market and more generally on markets as economic and cultural institutions. In 1997 she co-founded, with Judy Homan, The Friends of Central Market; between 1999 and 2000 she coordinated the Local Legacies Project Team for the Library of Congress and authored the original submission Central Market and the tradition of Market in Lancaster, Pennsylvania.

RICHARD K. KENT, Ph.D., is Professor of Art History at Franklin & Marshall College, where he teaches courses in East Asian art history and in the history of photography. Apart from his activity as a scholar of Chinese art, he has written poems and made photographs for several decades. His photographs have been shown in exhibitions at various museums, including the Griffin Museum of Photography, the Lancaster Museum of Art, the State Museum of Pennsylvania, and the Woodmere Art Museum.

MARJORY COLLINS (1912–1985) was a photographer for the United States Office of War Information (OWI). In her visits to Lancaster County during the early 1940s, she photographed many aspects of war-time life in the city, as well as in Lancaster's small towns and villages.

Artist and photographer MELISSA W. CARROLL, a native of Lancaster County, has fond childhood memories of downtown and Central Market. She is a fine art graduate of York Academy of Arts, York, Pennsylvania and currently works as a freelance artist, greeting card designer, and professional stock photographer.

GEMMA DE LA FUENTE is a partner in the architecture and design firm of Paden de la Fuente. Ms. de la Fuente holds a Bachelors and a Masters in architecture from the University of Pennsylvania. The firm's list of historic preservation projects includes work for the White House and the Department of the Interior. Paden de la Fuente's most recent effort involved the complete investigation and documentation of Lancaster's Central Market as well as the coordination and design of the ensuing four firm report. This document is now being used by the Central Market Trust, guiding their restoration and renovation of the structure.

HAMMEL ASSOCIATES ARCHITECTS is a Lancaster-based, regional firm, practicing primarily in Southeastern Pennsylvania that has participated in over six dozen National Register rehabilitation projects. Principal Kenneth D. Hammel AIA, a restoration architect with 32 years of experience in working with historic buildings, is the lead architect for the City-sponsored 2010 Central Market rehabilitation project. The Hammel team of architects is working closely with city representatives, the Central Market Trust, and standholders to preserve the best of the market, while providing infrastructure to sustain the market for decades to come.

COMMUNITY HERITAGE PARTNERS is a Lancaster-based firm of architects, town planners, preservation consultants, and development advisers dedicated to building the vitality of places and reconnecting people with the heritage of their built environment, their communities, and their landscapes. A long-time friend of Central Market, the firm's most recent contribution of services was an extensive set of design assessments and recommendations, as part of the Assessments, Guidelines, and Recommendations for Preservation and Development of the Central Market in 2007–09. In addition to their work with Central Market, Community Heritage Partners has served as architects and consultants for project planning, market operations management, preservation and development of markets and markethouses in Columbia, Carlisle, Sunbury, and York, Pennsylvania, and in Portland, Maine.

LANCASTERHISTORY.ORG formed from the merger of Lancaster County's Historical Society and President James Buchanan's Wheatland. Photographs from the photo collection of LancasterHistory.org proved an invaluable resource in presenting views of Central Market from the earliest days of photography.

Index